Assiniboine
(Nakóda)
Counting Book 11–20

VICKI BISBEE

Printed in the United States of America

ISBN 979-8-89114-227-5 (sc)
ISBN 979-8-89114-228-2 (e)

Library of Congress Preassigned Control Number: 2025920189

2025.09.24

MainSpring Books
5901 W. Century Blvd
Suite 750
Los Angeles, CA, US, 90045

www.mainspringbooks.com

Introduction

"Assiniboine" comes from the Anishinaabe word that translates to "cooks by use of stones." The Assiniboine call themselves "Nakóda."

The author is a member of the Fort Peck Assiniboine Tribe in Northeastern Montana. Vicki Bisbee, Nakóda name "Shunk Togaja Wiya" (Gray Wolf Woman) is a retired School Counselor who lives on the Fort Peck Reservation.

Great efforts are being made to revitalize the Assiniboine language on the Fort Peck Reservation and areas where Assiniboine reside. Fort Peck Community College on the Reservation has been instrumental in teaching the Assiniboine culture and rich language. This book is a wonderful counting book for any age. Symbols used for Assiniboine words have developed and changed over time. A team of individuals from Fort Belknap Indian Reservation, Fort Peck Indian Reservation and Indiana University developed the most recent Nakóda dictionary published in 2018. Their dedication in developing our traditional language is greatly appreciated.

In the Assiniboine language there are no words that start with the letters, or have the sounds of F, L, Q, R or V from the English alphabet. Letters are pronounced as follows:

C = always pronounced as "ch"

E or e = pronounced between 'bet' and 'bait'

Ǧ or ǧ, Ȟ or ȟ = like English G except with a "scraping" or "gargling" sound

I or i = like in 'pol<u>i</u>ce' (ee)

Š or š = always pronounced as "sh"

Zh = pronounced as in 'plea<u>s</u>ure'

Ą Į and Ų = pronounced like a, i, and u but with air passing through the nose, rather than the mouth, like the word "teen."

11

eleven

agé wąží

ahGAY wahZEE

12
(twelve)

agé nų́ba

ahGAY NOOMbah

13
thirteen

agé yámni

ahGAY YAHmnee

14

fourteen

agé dóba

ahGAY DOEbah

15

fifteen

agé záptą

ahGAY ZAHptah

16

sixteen

agé šákpe

ahGAY SHAkpay

13

17

seventeen

agé iyúšna

ahGAY eeYOOshnah

18

agé šaknóğą

ahGAY shawkNOgah

19

nineteen

agé nąpcúwąga

ahGAY nahpJOOwahngah

20

twenty

wikcémna núɓa

winkCHAYmna NOOMbah

About The Author

Vicki Bisbee is a retired School Counselor. Born and raised on the Fort Peck Indian Reservation, Vicki graduated from Poplar High School in 1975. She attended MSU-Northern and earned a bachelor's degree in business education (1980) and a master's degree in education, guidane and counseling. Both her parents attended boarding schools Her parents were wheat farmers. Her mother is Chippewa from Turtle Mountain reservation in North Dakota and her dad is Assiniboine. There was no Native American culture taught in school, but much of that had changed when Vicki returned to the reservation in 1992. In 1996, Vicki enrolled in Native American Studies at Fort Peck Community College and received her Indian name from the late Kenny Ryan. In 1997, she began her cultural journey by participating in her first Medicine Lodge in 1997, which finished in 2000. Vicki married Loren Bisbee (Turtle Mountain Chippewa) in 2007. They live in Wolf Point, Montana and enjoy time with two daughters (Angela Hale and Renee Waddoups), five grandchildren and one great granddaughter.

www.ingramcontent.com/pod-product-compliance
Lightning Source LLC
Chambersburg PA
CBRC090834120626
46547CB00009B/681